the hole in me since the day you died

the hole in me since the day you died

using art as a way of expressing grief

seven personal stories

Developed by

David Labrum

with

Margaret Gloster

Published by
The Center for Hospice and Palliative Care, Inc.
South Bend, Indiana

Contents

Foreword

Grief is a normal, natural process that people experience after the death of someone they love. However, it most often does not feel normal or natural at all, so grievers need to be assured that their feelings are okay. Grief also takes time to process, yet most grievers are encouraged not to talk about the death after a certain length of time, and get on with life. Displays of grief often make others feel uncomfortable, and people may even withdraw from the bereaved. Yet the ongoing support of others is what makes it possible for most people to eventually adjust to the death of someone they love.

Following the death of my twenty year old daughter Cindy in October 1985, grief became a perpetual part of my life. On a rainy fall day, my bright, beautiful daughter was killed instantly in a car accident. I was devastated, and a part of me died with her that day. At first, I was in a profound state of shock, which allowed me to make funeral arrangements and bury my child. As time went by, the shock lessened and the reality of her death became overwhelming. I lived in a deep state of depression for a very long time: How could she die so young, with so much promise, and so much to give the world? How could I possibly live without her and carry on with the plans we had both made together? I agonized endlessly over these thoughts and questions. Sometimes I wanted to die too, so that we could be together again, and be free of the pain.

Yet I also wanted to live, and something compelled me to move forward. I wrote letters to Cindy describing my life without her, remembering the life we shared, and to God, demanding answers and begging for relief from the anguish I felt. I read voraciously about surviving the death of a loved one, near death experiences, reincarnation and other spiritual beliefs about death and life. I started reaching out to others and sought counseling. I attended meetings of The Compassionate Friends, where I could freely share my feelings, and listen to the personal stories of those who had similar feelings. All of these were small, important steps in my healing process.

Several years after Cindy's death I was on a new path. Perhaps the most important thing I did for myself was return to school and earn a masters degree in counseling. Eventually, I found my way to The Center for Hospice and Palliative Care, where I worked as a grief counselor. My personal experience has allowed me to help mothers, fathers, husbands, wives, brothers, sisters and children deal with their grief.

As a grief counselor I knew that, although "talk therapy" was helpful to many grievers, there were those who needed another way to work through their grief. I was excited when David Labrum developed an art counseling program to enhance the therapy services that we offered. The seven individuals whose images are presented in this book were among the many participants involved in this program called "After Images." Working with David, they used their art as a way of connecting themselves to their grief. Their paintings and drawings became a tactile process in which they were able to express emotions too painful or too overwhelming to voice.

Their images gave me a glimpse into their world as they grieved and struggled to understand the implication of their loss. These individuals had not expected the death of their loved ones. Suddenly, they had to deal with an overwhelming experience of shock, disbelief, confusion, angst, and constant questioning. There was no preparation, no opportunity to complete unfinished business with their loved one, no chance to say good-bye, no last hug or kiss, no last chance to say I love you.

As I observed them gradually work through their grief over a period of weeks, months and years, I was in awe of their efforts. I was amazed at their visual perception, creating artwork that represented, to me, their courage in searching for understanding within themselves at such a tumultuous time. The work they did, evident in this book, is truly a tribute not only to their loved ones, but to each of them as well.

Carolyn Pritchard, M.S., L.M.H.C.
Former Coordinator for Bereavement Services
The Center for Hospice and Palliative Care, Inc.
South Bend, Indiana

Introduction

As an art counselor for the Bereavement Art Counseling Program, "After Images," I worked with the individuals whose art work is presented in this book. During their participation, I encouraged them to develop their creative abilities, to use their art as a way to express their grief.

I met with each one in the "After Images" art studio. They would work alone in the studio space with my support, creating their paintings and drawings throughout their involvement in our program. In time, it would become a safe and secure place where they could commit themselves openly and honestly to their grief within.

Having no prior art experience, they were uncertain of their ability to create art. I assured them that their art work and subsequent "visual stories" could evolve within this room. By providing the guidance and support they needed to get started in their art making, they quickly moved beyond their concerns and began exploring the various art materials, devising innovative art techniques to create images uniquely theirs.

As they attended their sessions, their confidence grew in their art making. I observed them as they improvised, finding ways of using the oil paint sticks, pastels and acrylic paints, in creating images that enabled them to experience their grief.

Their presence in the studio every week indicated to me that they were becoming aware of the potential and the power that their art held for them. They were experiencing a growing need to create their art work, to put on paper what they were encountering in their lives. It had become a viable process, a way to get in touch with themselves, to express emotions and feelings that were difficult to access in any other way.

They shared these images with me, which revealed those parts of themselves that were in such pain and so well hidden: feelings of anger, guilt, sadness and loneliness. Their art work, invoking memories, perceptions and expressions of their grief and their lost loved one(s) were entrusted with me. Knowing that they could rely on my support emboldened them to take greater risks in their art making, and by so doing, move deeper into their grief.

Returning to the studio to enact their "grieving ritual" became a familiar and necessary routine. These were the two hours they set aside just for themselves, focusing solely on their needs. Here in a protected environment, they grew to rely on their art making, knowing it connected them to their grief in a manageable way. Because of the significance of their work, I assured them that these sessions would be available for as long as they needed them. Some participated for six months and others for as long as two years.

After they finished their work in our program, I approached them about sharing their art work and experiences in this book. They agreed and were eager to see their images reach others outside the program for the first time. They were excited that their art work, created solely for their own needs and benefit, could now quite possibly serve others, their stories offering a unique insight and perspective into the grieving process.

To create this book, I asked them to select those images that held the most significance for them. Because of space constraints, they had the challenging task of choosing a small number of images from a larger body of their art work. When asked to submit written statements about each image, several referred to journal entries that they had written when they created their pieces, while others relied on their memories.

What you will encounter in this book are seven personal stories of people who used their art work as a way of exploring aspects of themselves in shaping, defining, and eventually transcending their experience of grief.

David Labrum, M. F. A., M.S. L.M.H.C.
Bereavement Art Counselor
The Center for Hospice and Palliative Care, Inc
South Bend, Indiana

seven personal stories

Don Collins I never felt such terror, sadness, and helplessness. That was the day that my nightmare began. On Friday, July 21, 2000, my daughter, Melissa and her fiancé Chris, were killed instantly in a car accident. A truck driver under the influence of cocaine, crossed the center line and hit their car head on.

The following Wednesday we buried Melissa and Chris together in a shared plot. I do not remember very much about that day, except that it was the last day that I was able to see, touch, and kiss my baby girl, my daughter Melissa.

Because of the senseless behavior of this man who killed Melissa and Chris. . . .

I'm under a death sentence. I think of Melissa's death all the time.

December 20, 2000: Five months after their deaths

I'm crying a river of tears, crying all the time. Will I ever stop?

January 17, 2001: A month later

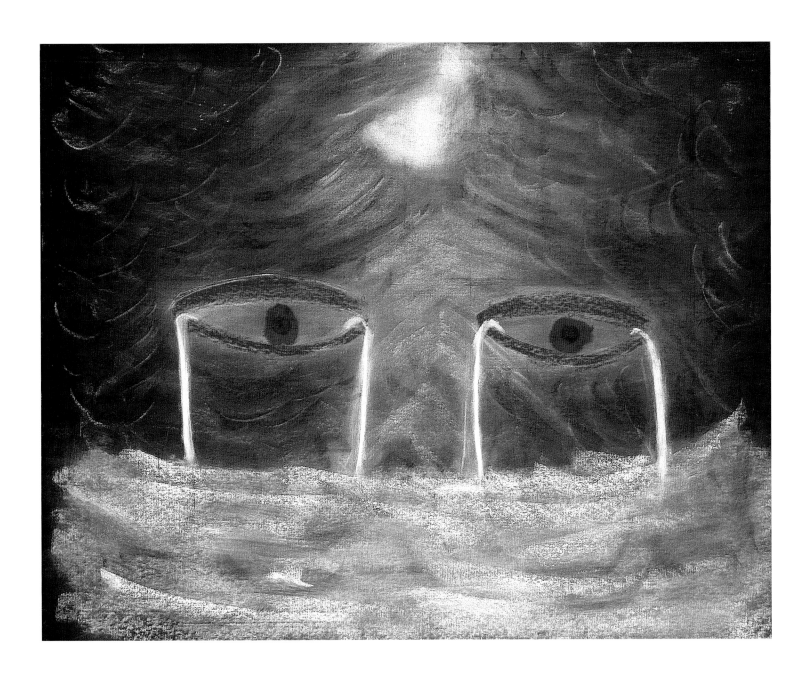

Another memory of Melissa's death comes crashing over me.

February 14, 2001: The next month

My hiding place—where I can escape and just be me.

My recurring thought is to die in order to be with Melissa.

March 7, 2001: The next week

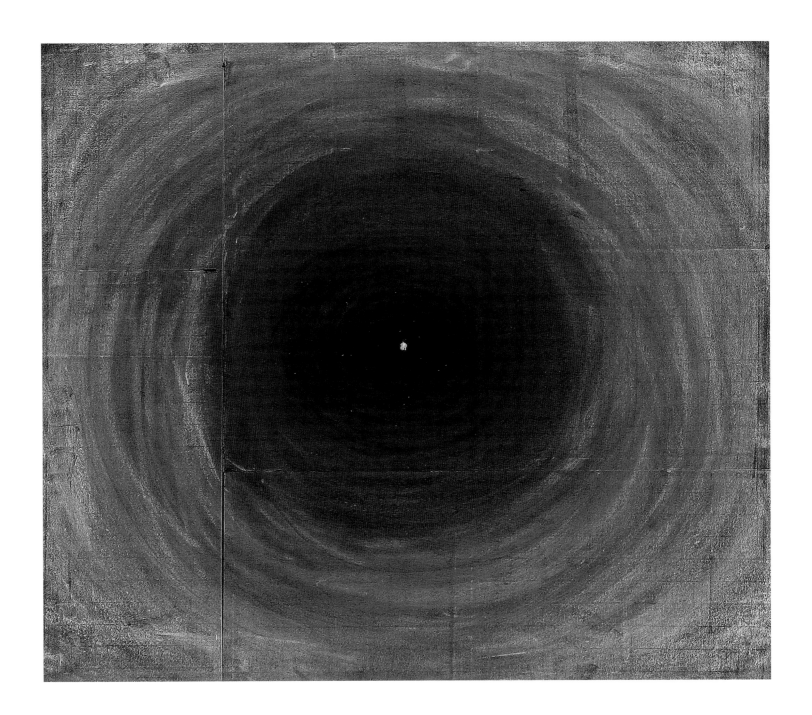

I'm safe in here — no thoughts, no worries about anyone. Not even Melissa.

My decision piece. Melissa's death could engulf me.
Do I want this?

Will Melissa always be part of me?

July 18, 2001: In another three months

I'm at Melissa and Chris's gravesite. Angry at God, but asking God to help me survive.

August 13, 2001: The next month

A door is closed in my life. The man who killed Melissa and Chris is finally sentenced today.

September 17, 2001: A month later

I'm better at handling my thoughts and feelings about Melissa.

October 5, 2001: In two weeks time

Will I make it though my suffering and pain? I'm fighting not to go back down.

October 24, 2001: After another three weeks

It's raining blood at the accident scene. I am facing my greatest fear. Did Melissa suffer? Did Chris suffer?

November 21, 2001: The next month

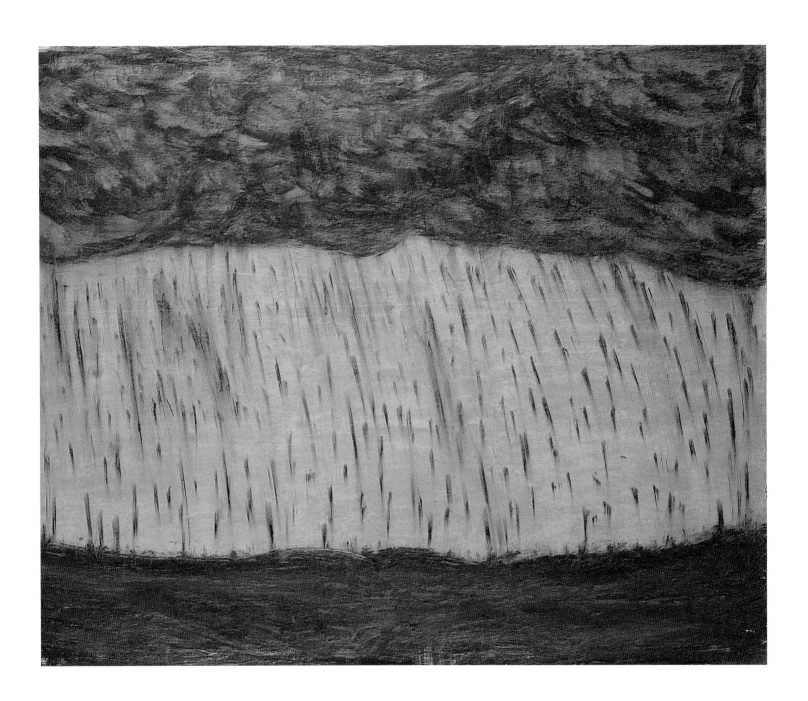

I won't let my anger toward the "evil man" who killed Melissa and Chris control my life.

November 28, 2001: The next week

Melissa is with me and I am with Melissa.

December 5, 2001: After another week

Melissa's hand is on my heart and Chris's is on my shoulder. It is reassuring to know that they are with me, comforting me in my grief.

December 19, 2001: Two weeks later

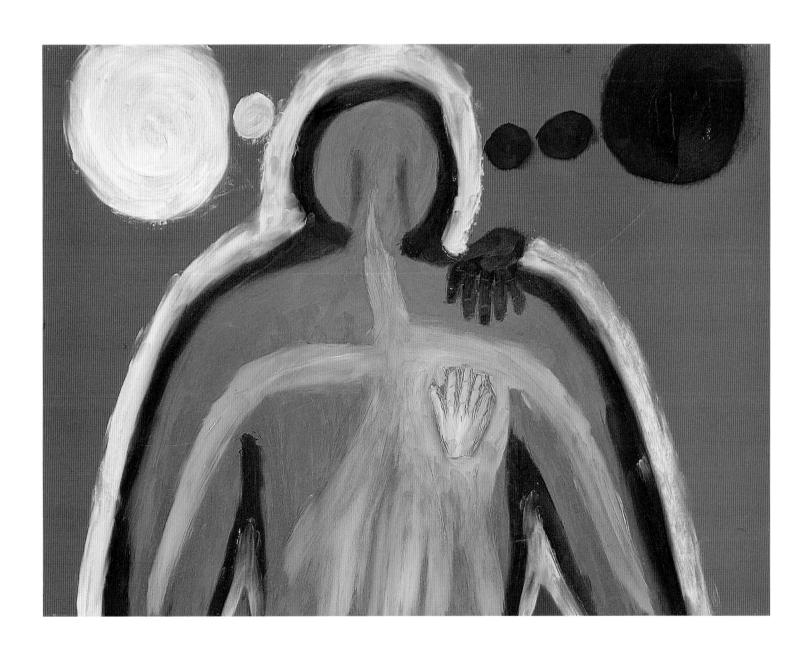

As I look back at my drawing, "Another memory . . . ," from two years ago, I remember those waves, so high and powerful, crashing into me from all directions, over and over again. The waves were my anger and bitterness of Melissa being taken away from me; my guilt, as her father I did not protect her and keep her safe; my rage at the man who killed Melissa and Chris; my fear of the accident scene, the carnage, pain, and blood.

With my drawing, "My decision piece . . . ," I made a determined effort not to let these waves overwhelm my life. I wanted to move beyond my thoughts about Melissa's death that were consuming me and causing me to doubt myself and the purpose of my life.

It was my "It's raining blood . . ." piece that helped me move forward in my life. After Melissa's death, I was tormented with thoughts of the accident scene, of what she might have experienced just before she died. I could not control these terrible thoughts until I had finally put them down on paper. In this drawing, I relived Melissa's death at the accident scene in every horrific detail. By imagining the worst and bringing it out into the open in this drawing for me to see, it somehow became less threatening and overwhelming. I was able to "conquer" that part of me that was so afraid. In time, these horrible images subsided.

I am choosing to move forward in my life. This tells me that I am starting to accept Melissa's death in some way. I can see her more clearly now, for she looks like my other three children. For so long after her death, I saw her as being larger than life. Perfect.

Moving forward does not mean that I will forget Melissa, or that I do not love her anymore—for I know she will always be with me.

Don Collins

January 16, 2004: Three years and six months after their deaths

Bill Wilson   My wife and I arrived home from our Florida trip on February 21, 2000. That night she developed a pain in her neck, which started her demise. I was not aware of the severity of her condition, and lost twelve valuable hours by not immediately taking her in for medical attention. If I had forced her to seek help, would the outcome have been different? Would she still be with me? I will never know. She died on February 23, 2000, at 5 pm from a brain hemorrhage.

After being married to Dianne for 35 years . . .

I am still fearful to draw anything recognizable. I cannot face her death.

June 27, 2000: Four months after her death

I cannot talk about the hole in my life.

July 6, 2000: After nine days time

Maybe there is hope?

July 18, 2000: Twelve days later

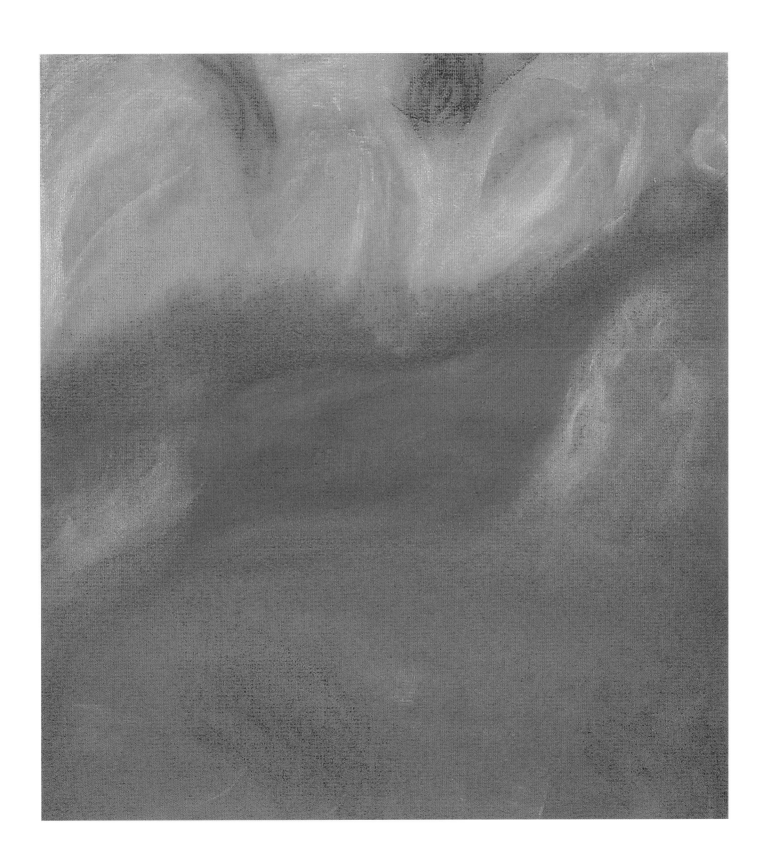

Is there a God? How could he do this to me!

August 8, 2000: Three weeks later

48

I am just trying to make it through each day.

September 1, 2000: After another two weeks

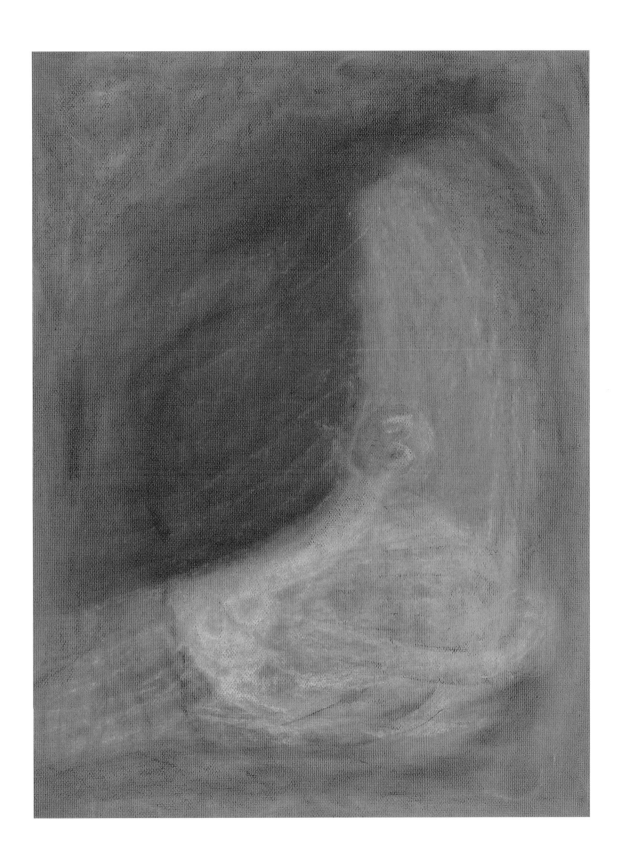

I don't know if there is a God, but damn it, Holy Mary, Mother of God, pray for me!

August 15, 2000: The next week

I want to be at home in Florida, but cannot go there alone. It is so empty now. I am scared to step though the doorway. What is on the other side?

September 22, 2000: Five weeks later

I feel so alone. As far as I can see—desolation.
I see no one!

October 3, 2000: After ten more days

I cannot bear to look at the anguish on the faces of the
people on the other side. It is more than I can take, so I
cover them up. Am I near the edge?

November 7, 2000: One month later

I wish I could climb out of my body. Let me out of here! This cannot be real!

November 29, 2000: In three weeks time

Am I going to make it?

December 6, 2000: One week later

All of a sudden the grim reaper just appeared. I have seen him before. I will see him again.

January 3, 2001: After another month

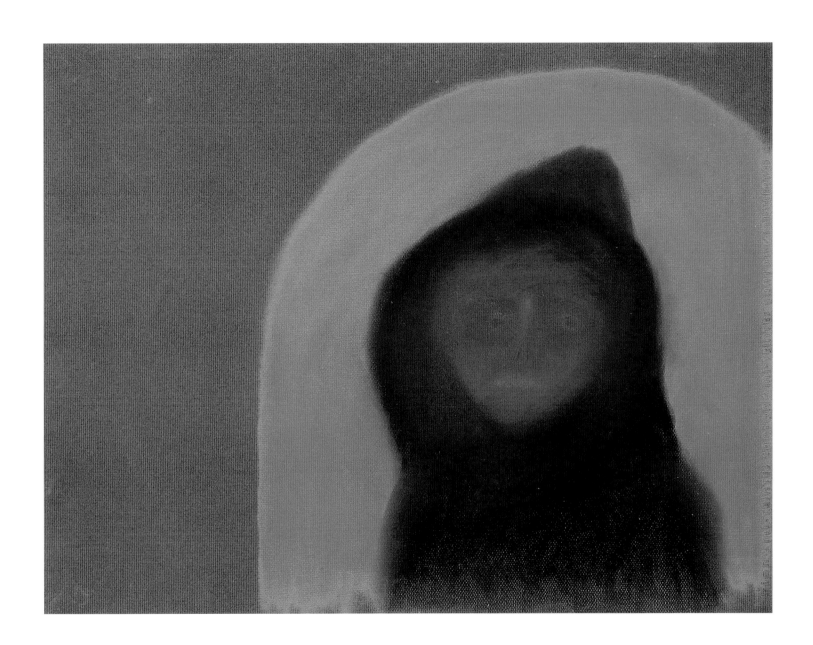

I feel like something is going to hit me very hard. I look forward to the force of the impact!

January 12, 2001: In a week and a half

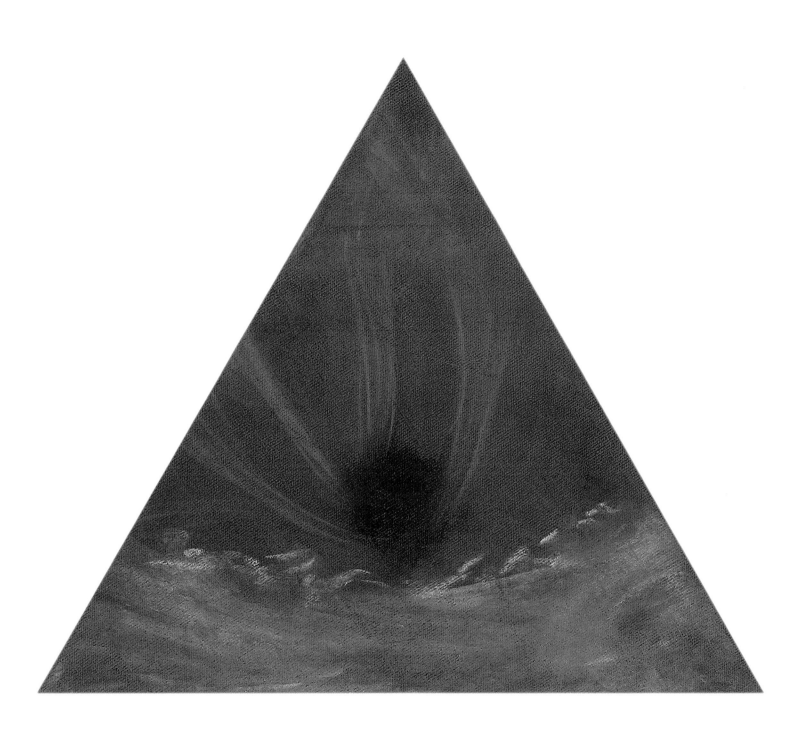

I feel like I could just explode with anger!

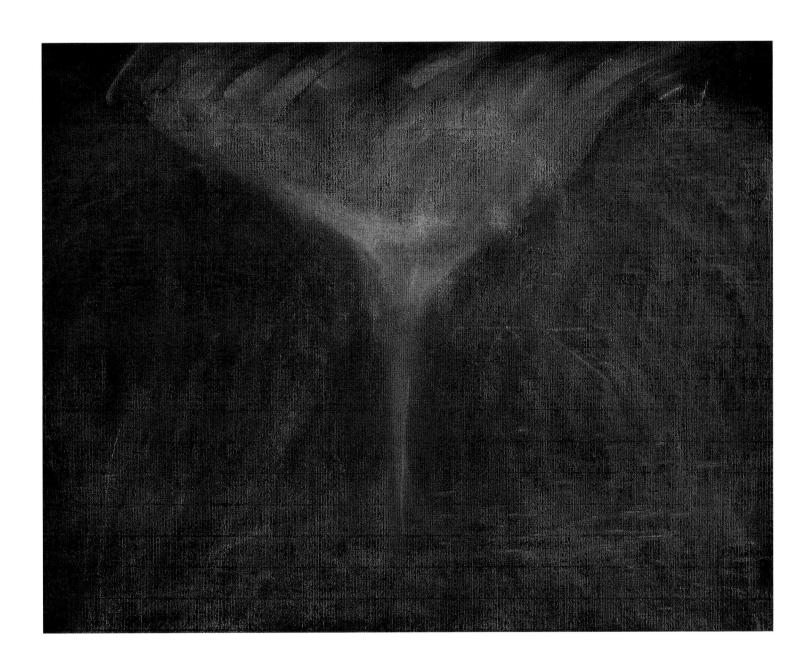

The colors of Dianne's dress.

I know there is a higher spirit inside my soul. I can feel the presence.

April 27, 2001: Over two months later

I remember starting my January 3, 2001, drawing with no image in mind. Choosing a violet piece of paper, I began rubbing pastel chalk over its surface. My hands and fingers began to move instinctively, my eyes darted back and forth, attempting to keep up with the marks I was making on the paper. One mark led to another and another; I became lost, absorbed in my work. Suddenly, an image appeared and I said, "I know who this is. This is the grim reaper! It is my image of death, of Dianne's death, and my fear of my own inevitable death."

Today, the image of the grim reaper is not as scary to me. I know he exists because I have learned life includes the eventual death of oneself. I am now able to face this ultimate issue of life. How my life ends and when it ends does capture part of my thoughts from time to time, but I do not dwell on it like I did four years ago.

The picture of the empty room with the golden cross above the doorway remains one of my favorite drawings. I call it "The Other Side." All one has to do is walk through the doorway and whatever comes after death awaits. Following Dianne's death, I became preoccupied with "the other side," asking myself, "Do I want to step through to the other side? Will I have the courage? Will I see God?"

Today what awaits me on the other side is just as mysterious to me, but I have no desire to find out.

Bill Wilson

March 10, 2004: Four years and one month after her death

Linda Mullenix   Our son Paulie was born on February 10, 1998, when David, our first son, was seven years old. He was born with several birth defects that his doctors assured us they could treat, and that he would be fine. After five months in the hospital, our son finally came home. Several months later, Paulie caught the flu and his heart gave up. We lost the battle that my husband and I fought so desperately to win. Our Paulie was gone.

Our third son Scottie was born February 9, 2000. He was perfect and beautiful. He brought joy and hope back to a family that was in so much pain. Then on a beautiful and sunny day in August, I received the phone call that no parent ever wants to get. They said Scottie had stopped breathing at his day care and was now in the hospital. He died before I could get there. He died from SIDS.

The death of my two sons, Paulie and Scottie, have changed my life forever. I will never be the same . . .

I am a bad person, I must be.   I am a bad mommy. I must have done something wrong to have Paulie and Scottie die.

January 16, 2002: Over three years after the death of Paulie
Nearly eighteen months after the death of Scottie

I can never again be who I was, and I don't want to be who I am.

You can no longer come into my very little world. It is too painful. The edges are too sharp, and it would be too hard for you.

February 27, 2002: After another three weeks

It is dark and the waves beat against my boat all the time. There are sharks all around, calling me to give up.

March 27, 2002: The next month

I want Paulie and Scottie back! I want to go back to the way my life was before. It is too hard for me to go forward!

April 17, 2002: In three weeks time

Since Scottie died, I have refused to cut my hair. I want to look the part when I am committed to the nut house. I flip my hair up over my face and rock in my chair. And do nothing.

April 23, 2002: The next week

I am tired of everyone telling me how I should feel and what I need. My life is like a bad dream that I never get to wake up from.

Is my story safe with anyone? So many people want
me to be who I was and to pretend it never happened.

June 12, 2002: In another month

I have played this game with myself for so long where I am a victim and stuck in this little world, waiting for someone to come and save me—you know, my husband, my mother, my friends, anyone. I am finally to the point where I know that I am the only one who can help myself.

August 21, 2002: After ten more weeks

I will let my children be in heaven. I know now that
I cannot hold them here with me, and they are not
coming back no matter how hard I pray.

September 25, 2002: In a months time

My David

My life is still very hard and every day is a struggle. I'm teaching myself how to live.

October 7, 2002: Two weeks later

I am starting over again without my medication, the pile of prescription drugs that I was taking for depression, anxiety, acid reflux. These drugs that helped me "survive" Paulie and Scottie's death are now holding me back, keeping me locked in a fog, numbing and freezing me in my grief.

Today, I can feel again! I can cry again!

November 26, 2002: In another six weeks

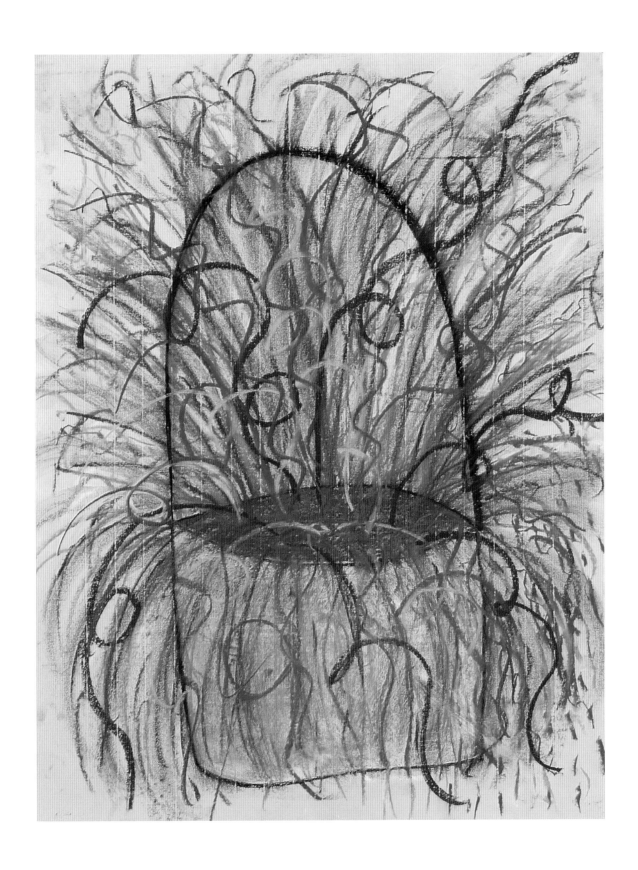

I want to be able to look back and say that I was proud of me, that I learned to live the life of a survivor even when all the odds were against me.

December 11, 2002: After two weeks

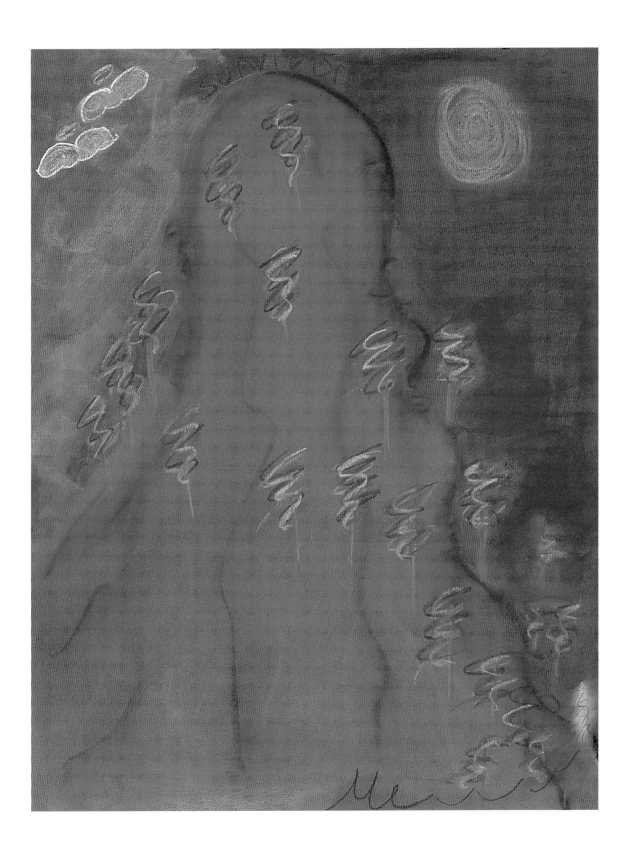

When I look back at my earliest drawing where I am hiding in the forest, I remember how hopeless I felt, how I wanted to give up and die. The forest, dark and scary, was the place where I could shut out the world and pretend that Paulie and Scottie were coming back. It is amazing to me that I was able to come out from such a place.

It is my drawing, ". . . when I am committed to the nut house . . . ," that challenged me to look deep within myself and my view of the world. After I finished this piece, I went home and cut my hair, the hair that I had refused to cut since Scottie's death. Cutting my hair symbolized my break with my desire of wanting to die or go crazy in order to stop my pain. I now knew that I could not change the past. By cutting my hair, I made the decision to begin to fight back, to come back to the living, to come back to myself.

For so long I held Paulie and Scottie against my chest, my heart, with everything I had. Today I no longer have to cling to them—their lives, their stories—during every waking moment of my life. Now, I'm able to put them down and let go of their hands, to let them play nearby, knowing that they will always come back to me, knowing that they will always be in my heart.

Linda Mullenix

March 17, 2004: Five years and six months after Paulie's death
Three years and eight months after Scottie's death

Greg Mullenix   My son Paulie was born with several birth defects and
lived at Riley Children's Hospital for the first five months of his life until July 12, 1998.
After that, he lived at home with us, his family. We cared for him until he died on
October 5, 1998.

When Scottie was born fourteen months later, we thought he would heal our wounds
after Paulie's death, but he was with us for only five short months. He left to be with
his brother in heaven on August 1, 2000.

After the deaths of my baby boys, I am . . . .

Numb. I'm a husk of a person.

February 7, 2002: Over three years after the death of Paulie
A year and a half after the death of Scottie

Paulie and Scottie

March 14, 2002: Five weeks later

Paulie

April 4, 2002: After another three weeks

Scottie

June 20, 2002: Over two months later

The second anniversary of Scottie's death.

August 1, 2002: In six weeks time

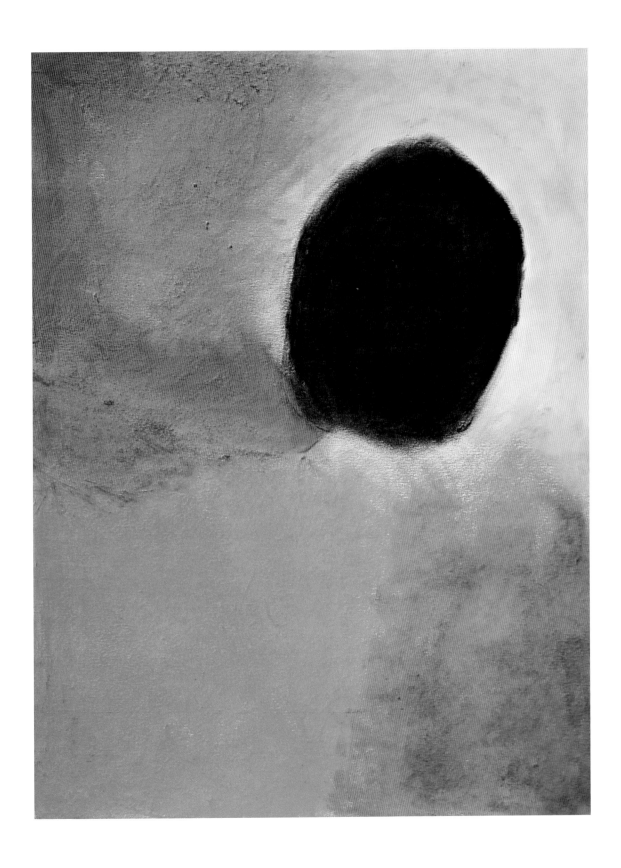

For a moment I am free from Paulie and Scottie's deaths.

August 29, 2002: Four weeks later

Everyone is afraid to hear Paulie and Scottie's stories. I am speaking into the ear of ignorance.

September 19. 2002: In another three weeks

I am releasing my babies, Paulie and Scottie. They are letting me go.

November 7, 2002: Seven weeks later

When I think of Scottie's short life, I feel deceived and cheated. I'm angry at life and God for letting Scottie die. I needed Scottie. And so did Linda and David. We were counting on him to help us take away our pain, to heal our wounds from losing Paulie.

Paulie always had physical problems since birth. I always knew that there was a chance that we might lose him. Because of this, I was able to accept his death in some way. But Scottie—he was perfect—there was nothing wrong with him.

Maybe I expected too much from Scottie's life.

Greg Mullenix

April 21, 2004: Five years and seven months after Paulie's death
Three years and nine months after Scottie's death

Kathy Carson   Our son Kyle was a junior, majoring in engineering at Valparaiso University, when he was killed in an automobile accident on January 18, 1998. Early on that day, Kyle, as president of his fraternity, had been very busy with the alumni weekend events including the basketball game. While he was at the game, some of the alumni started drinking back at the fraternity house. This was against the newly established rule that banned alcohol during this weekend. When Kyle returned from the game, he was faced with the difficult task of calling a house meeting because of these infractions and cancelling the remaining fraternity events for the weekend.

After this meeting, Kyle needed some time alone and took a drive in his truck. It was a clear, cold winter night with no snow. Kyle hit a patch of black ice and struck a utility pole on Highway 421. Our son died instantly.

Kyle is my shining star. I was always Kyle's mom.
That is all I ever wanted.

Nov. 7, 2002: Almost five years after his death

I'm still out on this lonely stretch of highway where Kyle died five years ago, searching for him, wanting to comfort him, protect him.

I'm so angry at his fraternity brothers "for worshiping alcohol," causing him to be out on that road, all alone!

December 12, 2002: The next month

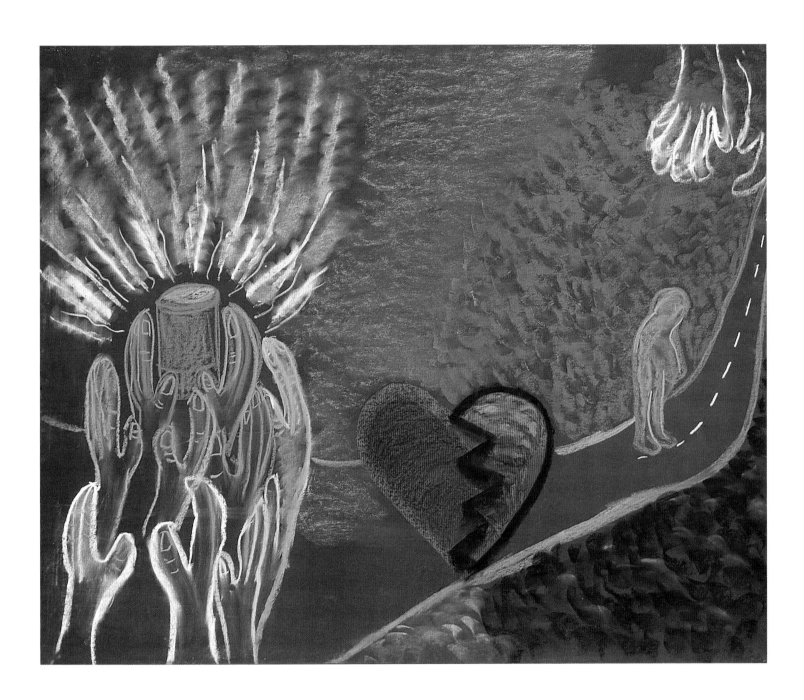

I'm jealous, angry, and hurt that my dreams for Kyle are gone—as I see other children's drea ms sail high in the breeze.

January 16, 2003: In another month

Since Kyle's death, I have had these horrible thoughts of him in his truck wrapped around that pole. For the first time I can see angels gathering Kyle in their arms, comforting him. And they are comforting me.

March 25, 2003: Over two months later

I am trying to stay with Kyle, going down as far as I can with him. But he is going deeper and entering a new and mysterious place.

April 17, 2003: In three weeks time

I am being told to move on. Am I ready to go on without Kyle?

May 1, 2003: After two weeks

How far have I come? Do I still need to retreat to my safe place, my rock garden, where I am not lonely or sad, where life is as it should be, where Kyle never died?

I cannot hold back nor deny Kyle's death any longer.

June 5, 2003: In three weeks time

For five years I held on to Kyle so tight, tugging on him, pulling him back to me, telling him that he was not free to go.

I am saying goodbye to Kyle now. I am letting him go.

My old path was made up of anger, bitterness, and self-pity—that led me nowhere.

I'm laying flagstones for a new path, a "new normal" life for me.

July 3, 2003: In two more weeks

I am moving on in my life, and not just for Kyle anymore.

July 17, 2003: Two weeks later

I am making decisions about my life . . . expanding in new directions.

August 7, 2003: After three weeks

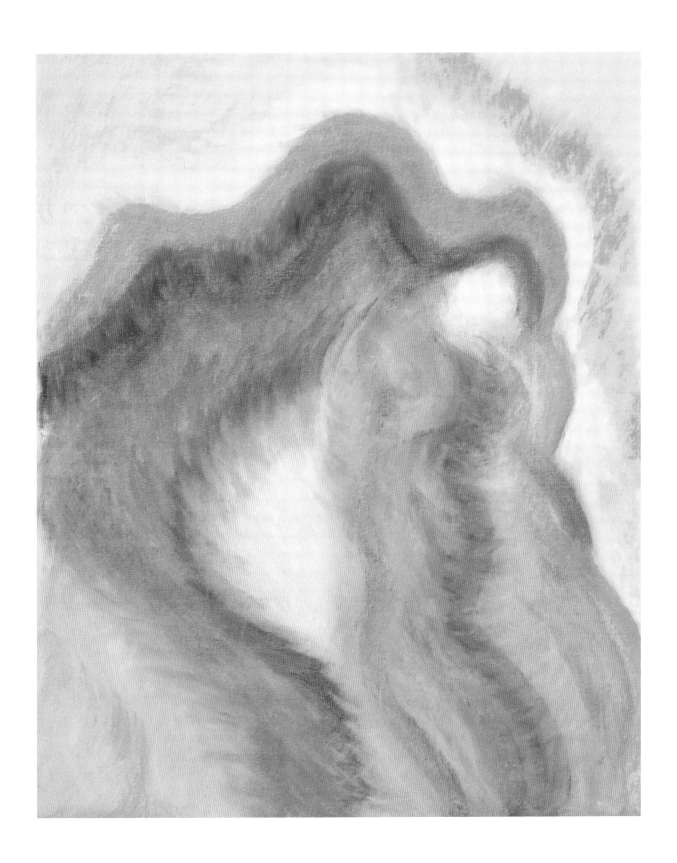

I don't see my drawing, "Kyle is my shining star . . . ," in the same way today. My attention now is on the three yellow stars that were not as bright or as significant to me then as they are now. It is painful for me to look back and see that I was not there for my son Gavin, my daughter Kelly, and my husband Scott when they were hurting, when they needed support. I was so preoccupied with Kyle back then—so consumed by my own needs, unable to realize that I had shut out the most important people in my life.

My drawing, ". . . my safe place . . . ," remains unfinished today. It remains so because I no longer need my rock garden in the same way that I did before. It was a place I would retreat to in order to hold onto Kyle, to reflect on only warm and happy memories, a dream-like place where life is as it should be, where Kyle never died.

I no longer have to go to my safe place to deny Kyle's death or to shut out the world. I am stronger than that today, for I have faced my greatest fear—my fear of losing one of my children, my son Kyle. I have survived.

Today when I go to my safe place, I seek out my son Kyle to tell him how much I miss him, how I am feeling stronger and more excited about my life today.

Kathy Carson

_____

March 30, 2004: Six years and two months after his death

Laurie Schuster   April 6th, 2000, we were a happy family on vacation—laughing, enjoying each other as we contentedly floated down the river. I saw the basketball-sized rock as it fell. I heard the sound it made when it crushed my husband's skull. In the moment it took to shout "Mike!" our lives were forever changed.

The hours following the accident were nightmarish. We were not allowed to be at Mike's side the next day when he died in the Mexican hospital. How could our contented, happy life turn into a maelstrom in the blink of an eye?

Wretched, raw, searing, gaping wound. Deep in the recesses of my heart and gut. My grief sits there, a heavy weight waiting to devour me.

October 9, 2001: Eighteen months after his death

Dark, hollow, empty. Part of me wants to wrap myself in a cocoon and lock the world out. Part of me wants to fly and be free. I feel so separated from the rest of the world.

November 6, 2001: The next month

How can I take control of life again? How can I grasp
some stability? I'm trying to mold my life, but I don't
know what to do. I'm split between how I really feel
inside and what I let people see.

December 11, 2001: In five weeks time

Reshaping, remolding, rebuilding with bits and pieces of what is left. How do you make sense out of something that makes no sense at all? How do you rebuild something that can't be rebuilt? How do you move forward and not lose your past?

January 22, 2002: After six weeks

Frustrated, explosive anger! Everything is out of my control! I'm so tired of coping. I'm so tired of presenting the appearance of "doing well." I just want my normal life back!

February 19, 2002: In another month

Shifting, moving, evolving. Going somewhere and yet nowhere. Constant motion and emotion.

February 26, 2002: One week later

I surround the deep and inner pain with a buffer of outer calm. I have to protect and contain it amidst all the confusion. I can't stand to lose any more of me.

March 12, 2002: After two weeks time

My emotions flow liquid like a river, churning through the bleak, dark, rough rapids, and painfully choking passages—stretching, searching for smoother waters. I go with the flow, wondering where it will end.

April 23, 2002: In six more weeks

Coagulation. The wound remains, yet growth is possible. I will always carry this deep pain, but I am finding a way to live with it.

May 7, 2002: After another two weeks

I have traveled through the darkest anguish, the rawest pain, and continued forward, choosing to rebuild. I have options.

May 28, 2002: Three weeks later

For me, part of my grief was this horrible feeling of having no control over my life today compared to my previously wonderful, stable life. Mike had been violently ripped away, and a part of me went with him.

One of my first drawings revealed to me the raw and gaping wound Mike's death left in me. I felt that my raw pain would devour me if I could not find a way of stopping it from festering. I felt this wound deep inside me, but this was the first time that I saw it.

I had been trying to work around my wound, pretending that it didn't exist, hoping it would just stop hurting. By making it tangible on paper, I could no longer ignore its existence. After time, and many oily fingers later, I was able to take my wound and see it coagulate with new growth.

This deep pain will always be a part of me. It will never heal, it will never stop hurting, but it no longer controls me. I found a place inside me to contain my wound.

Once I stopped the festering, I began to move forward in my life

Laurie Schuster

February 8, 2004: Three years and ten months after his death

Mary Molnar   My son Eric was seventeen and a second semester senior at Marian High School. On Valentine's Day, February 14, 2002, he was driving to a friend's house after school when he lost control of his car, left the road, and hit a tree. He was killed instantly. That evening my husband and I had the difficult task of telling our other children that Eric had died. This was one of the hardest things we have ever had to do.

We spent the next few days picking out a casket, cemetery plot, and planning Eric's funeral. Eric's friends drifted in and out of our home. Our family was with us. We were going through the motions of living. His funeral was the following day, President's Day. It was appropriate for my son, the gentleman and the quiet leader that he was.

I feel so lonely and empty, missing you. Yet I know
that your death will never sever the bond between us.

September 23, 2002: Seven months after his death

I am spiraling downward. My despair and sadness leave me little energy. Will I always feel this way?

October 14, 2002: Three weeks later

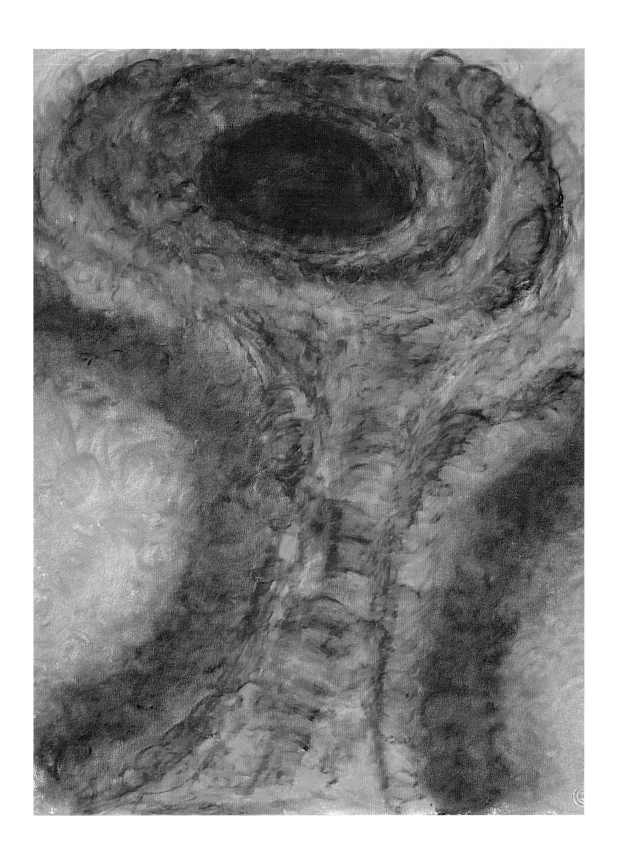

I was hoping that they had made a mistake. The first thing I noticed was your favorite scarf. It was you.

Nov. 18, 2002: After another month

I relived that day over a thousand times, thinking I could change it and bring you back.

February 14, 2003: Three months later; the first anniversary

I am engulfed in turmoil. It seems like there is no way out.

April 14, 2003: After another two months

How do I get to where I'm going?

May 5, 2003: In three weeks time

Eric, you looked so handsome and grownup when you wore your suit to the dance. My heart ached when I took it to the funeral home for you to wear. I remember worrying that you would outgrow it before graduation.

June 23, 2003: Six weeks later

I am asking God why, knowing that there is no
answer. If I could make some sense out of losing you,
it would make it easier for me to go on.

August 18, 2003: After almost two months

My days are dark and full of sadness. I miss your face, your smile.

September 15, 2003: A month later

I am getting the poison out of me! I'm still so full of anguish. It keeps me from seeing the good possibilities that life can bring.

November 10, 2003: Nearly two months later

I catch a glimpse of light in the midst of darkness. My anger keeps me from moving toward it.

December 8, 2003: In another month

I have survived two years without you. I am stronger than I realize.

February 14, 2004: Two months later; the second anniversary

My love for you my son remains deeper and stronger than ever.

February 24, 2004: In ten days time

Today, I experienced love and kindness from people I have never met before. Somehow this makes me feel closer to you.

March 2, 2004: After another week

There has been a hole in me since the day you died. I experience moments of peace and joy in my life. Yet the hole remains.

April 6, 2004: The next month

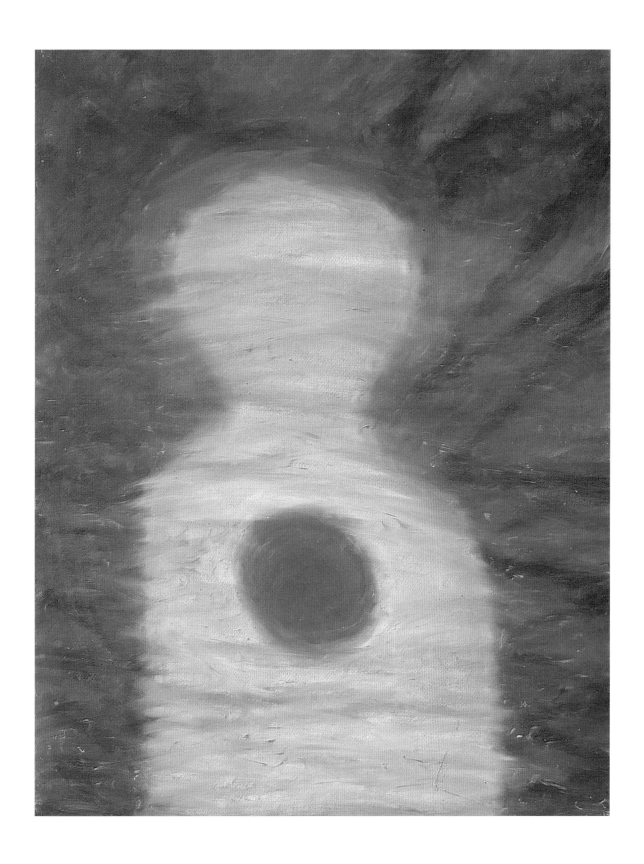

In the beginning, my artwork focused on Eric's life, the accident scene, and his funeral. Then as the months went by, I began to focus on myself. I began to put my feelings down on paper. There were times when I felt that there was not a piece of paper large enough to contain all of them. I felt myself evolving as an artist for I was able to identify with greater clarity in my art work, the fear, anger, and deep sadness that dwelled deep within me. I grew accustomed to having time in the studio each week to be alone, to get my fingers dirty with the oil pastels. It was this time in the studio that I could be with Eric if I wanted to, or I could be totally alone.

My most significant art piece is my portrayal of myself, showing the large hole that Eric's death has left inside me. I have always sensed that this hole was inside me since the day he died, but it was not until two years later that I was really ready to see it. I could now acknowledge that Eric died and is not coming back.

I have always known that losing Eric could destroy me. I could have withdrawn and just quit living. But instead I have made my decision to move on with my life, learning to live without Eric and with the hole in me that can never be filled.

Mary Molnar

May 28, 2004: Two years and three months after his death

afterwords

When I was working on a drawing I felt like I had my feelings in my fingers, my palms,
my hands. I squeezed them, wrestled with them, punched them!
It was a way for me to fight back!

Don Collins

The worst part of my grief was my loneliness, I was so alone I was not here.

My artwork helped me to see myself again.

Bill Wilson

For many years, I slept in order to escape Paulie and Scottie's deaths.
My artwork forced me to be awake with myself and my thoughts, focusing on what
was real and what was not.

Linda Mullenix

I used my art to express feelings that I could not put into words.

Greg Mullenix

My artwork always told me a story about myself that I did not know before.

Kathy Carson

Sensing the texture of the oil pastels as my fingers pushed, pressed and swirled against the paper, enabled me to physically grasp my feelings and take control.

Laurie Schuster

Being in the studio again, "alone with my art," provided sustenance to that part of me that was lost without him.

Mary Molnar

Acknowledgments

I wish to express my thanks to these individuals who were instrumental in the making of this book: Margaret Gloster, designer and production coordinator, whose tutelage and continual efforts brought this book to fruition; Barbara Searle, creative consultant, whose counsel and ideas helped shape this book; David Hugus, photographer, who produced the original manuscript and whose indispensable efforts made this book possible.

Special thanks go to M. Orgo, production consultant, and editorial advisors Mike Knaack, Judy Kelly, and John Raymer.

Deep appreciation also goes to Carolyn Pritchard for writing the foreword and for her guidance in helping me construct the statements for the seven stories.

I want to thank the following individuals who were involved with this book: Tom Spencer, Sam Oliver, Sam Marvel, Kathy Mow, Peg Maupin, Mickey Lane, and Carlye Reimer.

My gratitude is extended to Mark Murray, President/CEO; Roberta Spencer, Director of Support Services; and Liz Lamon, Bereavement Coordinator—all from The Center for Hospice and Palliative Care—for giving me the opportunity to create this book.

I am grateful to Jean Logan, Exhibition Coordinator for the School of the Arts Gallery, Indiana University, South Bend, Indiana, for her support of The Center for Hospice and Palliative Care's art exhibition, "Transcending Loss," in 2002. The enthusiastic community response to this exhibit served as the impetus for this book.

My gratitude also goes to the following individuals who helped obtain the underwriting support of their organizations for the "After Images" program: Rick Strickland and Karen Sommers of Memorial Health Systems, South Bend, Indiana, and Debra Bruce Janicki of the Indiana Arts Commission, South Bend, Indiana.

And finally, love and thanks to my wife Dana for her contribution to this book, as well as for her unwavering support and encouragement during the "three year odyssey" of putting it together.

Colophon

Published by The Center for Hospice and Palliative Care, Inc.
Book Copyright © 2005 David Labrum
Designed by Margaret Gloster
Printed and Bound by Imago
First Edition, 2005

The Center for Hospice and Palliative Care, Inc., 111 Sunnybrook Court, South Bend, Indiana
46637, Telephone (574) 243-3100, Fax (574) 243-3134. For information on purchasing this
book contact the publisher at www.centerforhospice.org.
David Labrum can be contacted at www.dplabrum.com
or by telephone at (574) 850-7257

ISBN 0-9769182-0-X
Printed in Singapore by Imago